Journal

YOUR WAY TO RETIREMENT

EVOLVE INTO RETIREMENT
IT ISN'T JUST ABOUT THE MONEY
BE THE ARCHITECT OF YOUR LIFE

JOAN MARIE GAGNON

BALBOA
PRESS
A DIVISION OF HAY HOUSE

Balboa Press books may be ordered through booksellers or by contacting:

Balboa Press
A Division of Hay House
1663 Liberty Drive
Bloomington, IN 47403
www.balboapress.com
1 (877) 407-4847

Because of the dynamic nature of the Internet, any web addresses or links contained in this book may have changed since publication and may no longer be valid. The views expressed in this work are solely those of the author and do not necessarily reflect the views of the publisher, and the publisher hereby disclaims any responsibility for them.

The author of this book does not dispense medical advice or prescribe the use of any technique as a form of treatment for physical, emotional, or medical problems without the advice of a physician, either directly or indirectly. The intent of the author is only to offer information of a general nature to help you in your quest for emotional and spiritual well-being. In the event you use any of the information in this book for yourself, which is your constitutional right, the author and the publisher assume no responsibility for your actions.

Any people depicted in stock imagery provided by Thinkstock are models, and such images are being used for illustrative purposes only.
Certain stock imagery © Thinkstock.

ISBN: 978-1-5043-7222-0 (sc)
ISBN: 978-1-5043-7223-7 (e)

Library of Congress Control Number: 2016921459

Print information available on the last page.

Balboa Press rev. date: 10/17/2017

**Dedicated to my parents
Robert and Genevieve Gagnon**

PREFACE

Tell me a fact, and I'll learn.
Tell me a truth, and I'll believe,
but tell me a story and
it will live in my heart forever.
Indian Proverb

I recently retired as a financial planner, and the transition was not as easy as I thought it would be. I have studied financial transitions for many years, but, wow, when it came to my own changeover, I was surprised at the many emotions that took over. Being a financial advisor, I would not have retired if money were an issue. But I could have prepared better for the "other" issues.

So why didn't I journal about retirement five years prior to that day? It's because I thought retirement for me was mostly just about the money. I am here to tell you: it isn't.

Although I am sure the second half of life would have eventually evolved wonderfully, I wanted to speed up the process of getting to the perfect retirement. "Aha!" I started journaling daily about retirement. That's when I felt compelled to share these "aha" moments with you. You too will have many of these as you journey through this book.

It is my heartfelt desire for you to obtain clarity on all the various aspects of retirement: the good, the bad, and, yes, the ugly. This book will provide you with questions you can journal about or just think about to obtain that clarity and action steps to move forward.

Enjoy the journey.

ACKNOWLEDGEMENTS

Writing this book has been such a wonderful, fulfilling experience. And many people have contributed and supported me throughout this process.

My dear husband, Jim, has been so supportive. I have taken what I call "writing vacations" so I could concentrate on my book. He lovingly understood that I needed this time and space.

I am deeply grateful to my writing book club members—Karen Benz, Marietta Courtney, Wendy Juergens, Jen Vondenbrink, and Tina Walsh—for giving me encouragement and structure to complete this first book.

I joyfully acknowledge Wendy Hanson, my business coach of many years, who helped me through the thought processes of this idea of *Journal Your Way To* series when it was just a twinkle in my eye.

My dear friend and editor, Jean Sirois, deserves many thanks and praises for her patience and quick turnarounds so I could meet my deadlines.

The dedication and professionalism my graphic guy, Calvin Nelson, and the web designer, Monica Bentley, displayed was over the top.

And last but not least, I warmly acknowledge my family, friends, and clients who critiqued many of the questions ahead of time for me. Their honesty and encouragement were priceless.

CONTENTS

INTRODUCTION

It is thought and feeling which guides the universe, not deeds.
Edgar Cayce

If you picked up this book, you probably know the benefits of journaling or have been curious about it. If you don't have experience with journaling, you are in for a life-changing experience. I have been journaling off and on for twenty-five years. It has given me clarity on ideas, life, and love—when I needed it.

Retiring from the workforce, specifically from the daily routine you have known for many years, can be scary, exciting, frightening, calming, or paralyzing. This book will guide you through thought processes that may or may not have entered your mind as you begin to think of retirement several years away or if you are fast approaching your last day in the workforce that you currently know. This book will also be helpful if you are retired, but you have not assimilated into your new life comfortably.

The subconscious and conscious minds together are potent resources that can give us just what we need to have a wonderful, happy next phase of our life. By asking yourself reflective questions, the real truth will be revealed. What you think and believe has a profound impact on your world.

The journal questions will bring you from how you are feeling today to how you want to feel when you retire. It will help you blend the logical mind and your emotions.

This book will not address financial numbers in detail but will bring out into the open your feelings about your financial goals after you leave the workforce. Think of the journaling as a personal, private conversation with yourself about retirement.

JOURNAL
YOUR WAY

THE POWER OF THE BRAIN

Your vision will become clear only when you can look into your own heart. Who looks outside, dreams; Who looks inside, awakes.
Carl Jung

For most people, retirement is a joyful happening. But even for those lucky, joyful retirees, they are going to go through a transition in their lives that could be a game changer.

Understanding the brain can be powerful when emotions surface before and during retirement. If thinking about leaving the workforce brings on a high level of stress, then taking steps to reduce that tension is imperative. Imagine the person who is forced into retirement earlier than planned. The stress level will potentially be off the charts.

If chronic stress is not managed, the brain goes into basic survival mode rather than logical, productive, long-term thinking. The result of this could show up in loss of memory, fatigue, blood sugar imbalance, higher blood pressure, and a decrease in overall health. Sounds extreme, doesn't it?

The ideal situation is to plan before retirement to keep the brain from going into survival mode. I can tell you, when I first retired, I experienced many of the above symptoms. I don't want to promise that, if you contemplate all the questions in this journal, you won't experience retirement stress. That would be irresponsible. I just want you to recognize various reactions you may experience physically. Recognizing these reactions will help move you faster into a joyous retirement. And working through the questions in this book may help you evolve into the next chapter of your life faster.

Henriette Anne Klauser wrote in her book *Write It Down, Make It Happen*, "'Good Happens' is the philosophy behind this book, my premise is the overriding belief that good things happen and that life is a narrative you have a hand in writing." In other words, you still have the power to create the perfect retirement. Just by writing down your thoughts about retirement, you will be way ahead because your subconscious will start the ball rolling in your favor. Watch for it! It will happen. I promise you. Have you ever written down your five-year goals and then filed them in a cabinet? Five years later, you find the goal sheet, and you have accomplished many of those objectives. That was not by chance.

Dr. Joe Dispenza, the author of *Breaking the Habit of Being Yourself*, says, "Our thoughts can become our experience." Neuroscience is proving every day that our minds are very powerful. And recently it has been confirmed that our digestive systems are connected to our brains. I'm not going to go on and on about these topics because I want you to start your retirement journaling sooner rather than later. At the back of the book, I listed resources regarding these findings.

You do not have to have a humdrum retirement. Journal it; live it.

Starting now …

JOURNAL
YOUR WAY

HOW TO UTILIZE THIS BOOK

Things do not happen. Things are made to happen.
John F. Kennedy

Attitude and Intention

Your attitude and intention around these journal questions matter greatly. I want to emphasize that you do not have to journal. Just asking yourself and your partner these questions can be helpful in getting to that perfect retirement. You can utilize the space in this book, or you can purchase a nice spiral-bound journal to set the tone that you are serious about this journey.

Journaling your thoughts can bring up feelings that have an impact on your being. As you write your way through these questions, be prepared to feel calm, joyful, ecstatic, sad, mad, and sometimes overwhelmed. These emotions can then make their way to your physical being. For instance, if you are writing about something that makes you mad, you could end up with a stomachache.

Don't throw in the towel when these physical symptoms show up. I'm mentioning it to you now because subconsciously you may stop journaling since it seems you always get a headache or stomachache during or after that journal session. This is normal. Persevere.

Some of the journal questions may be thought-provoking and may conjure up some old memories or fears. If they do, then yay! The journaling is working.

Date Your Journaling

It will be interesting to see how things change after a few weeks or months of journaling. Also it will be fascinating in years to come when you are living the life of your dreams and you revisit this journal. It will be great to see the progress and how writing gave you clarity to make your dreams come true. You will be able to see and celebrate your progress.

How Often You Should Journal

How often you journal really is up to you. Some people want to plow through these questions, while others want to contemplate each inquiry for a week. I recommend you test it out for yourself. If you do one question per day but are still thinking of that query when you are three questions further along, it might make sense to slow down a bit.

Worksheets / Meditations

Periodically I will reference the availability of a worksheet to help you organize your thoughts. The worksheets will be great for people who like to keep lists. Journaling in the space provided is still fine if you don't like worksheets.

I've included some guided meditations to go deeper. The Litmus Test especially is a wonderful tool to utilize the rest of your life.

JOURNAL
YOUR WAY

REFLECTIONS ON RETIREMENT TODAY

The blend of logic and emotion is the reality we live in.
Susan Bradley

What three words describe what retirement means to you, for example, relaxed, bored, organized, scared, and so on? Choose one word at a time to contemplate. What pictures come to your mind when you say that word? How do you feel when you say that term? Does someone else come to mind when you say that word or expression? Do you see yourself in a special room or home? Is the word grandiose, simple, depressing, uplifting, boring, or exciting? What is that all about?

Ask yourself these questions for each word you choose. For example, for calmness, I envision waking up each day without the alarm, not rushing off to the office for a crazy schedule. I let each day evolve. I will have a leisurely morning watching the morning news, drinking coffee, and reading the paper. I am very happy and calm.

Date: _____

_____

_____

_____

_____

_____

_____

_____

_____

_____

_____

_____

_____

_____

_____

_____

_____

_____

_____

_____

_____

_____

_____

_____

_____

_____

_____

_____

_____

_____

_____

_____

_____

_____

Yesterday was not your defining moment.
The calendar moved forward; why not you?
Steve Maraboli

The first journal question got your creative juices flowing about retirement in a different way. It wasn't about what you are going to *do* in retirement, but about how you *feel* about this phase of your life. Big difference!

If you are having trouble getting started, try to set a special time of the day or week for journaling. When I first started many years ago, I had to truly force myself. I thought it was a waste of valuable time. But as I pressed ahead, I recognized the value of journaling.

In fact, Abraham Lincoln, Thomas Jefferson, and many other United States presidents wrote in their journals every day! It is a great way to clarify your thoughts, plan, and create.

So describe a typical week for you when you retire. Start with Monday and then go day by day. Be very thorough. Include all activities—even paying bills, housekeeping, cutting the lawn, knitting, or chopping wood—and the people you will be with during the week.

Date: _____

_____

_____

_____

_____

_____

_____

_____

_____

_____

_____

_____

_____

_____

_____

_____

_____

_____

_____

_____

_____

_____

We keep moving forward, opening new doors, and doing new things, because we're curious and curiosity keeps leading us down new paths.
Walt Disney

You may have done a great job saving for retirement, but do you know what you'll be doing to fill your days? The majority of retired people never gave this much thought before they left the workforce. Most people envision their retirement will be like their vacation times. This can lead to boredom, sickness, and even depression when reality sets in.

I've interviewed many retired people, and all have different experiences regarding time frames to when they truly felt retired, ranging from three months to five years. You may need time to ponder this question. At the end of the journal, I will prompt you to come back to this question to fill in any blanks or rearrange your new busy calendar.

Describe the first twelve months of your retirement by month. For example, if you retire in June, what will that month look like as far as activities, projects, people you will see, and so on? Then give each month a theme. April could be "spring cleanup," and August could be "family vacation."

Date: _____

_____

_____

_____

_____

_____

This pouring thoughts out on paper has relieved me. I feel better and full of confidence and resolution.
Diet Eman

You are on the fourth *Journal Your Way to Retirement* question. We are currently journaling how we feel "today" about retirement. As you move on in the book, you will get more prolific in answering some of the blanks or blocks you may be running across.

So how do you like journaling? Are you experiencing any aha moments? Here are some benefits to journaling:

- It is a great GPS for what you want in retirement. Think about how much easier it is to take a trip across the country (retirement) when you have a GPS (journal) by your side.
- It will be a chronicle of your evolution toward an awesome retirement.
- It can unlock creativity and identify blocks you never gave any thought to.
- It can increase your realization of the future and even reduce stress.
- It can be the catalyst to action. We all know the power of brainstorming.

The following questions revolve around health:

- How is your physical and mental health today?
- Would your health be better in retirement? How and why?
- Would your health be worse in retirement? How and why?

Date: _____

_____

_____

_____

_____

_____

_____

_____

_____

_____

_____

_____

_____

_____

_____

_____

_____

_____

_____

_____

The biggest adventure you can take is to live the life of your dreams.
Oprah Winfrey

Describe your current home. Is it affordable, comfortable, small, large, a money pit, and so on? Elaborate on that description.

How long do you want to live in this home? Why? What characteristics do you like about your home? What are the negatives regarding staying in your home during retirement? What are the positives regarding staying in your home during retirement?

Do you want to move to another home? Why? Where? Do you feel like you are stuck staying in your home for various reasons such as money, family, health, and so forth?

What does your partner think about it? Do your attitudes differ on the subject? Is there room for compromise?

Date: _____

_____

_____

_____

_____

_____

_____

_____

_____

_____

_____

_____

_____

_____

_____

_____

_____

_____

_____

_____

_____

JOAN MARIE GAGNON

**Dissatisfaction (restlessness) is not a bad
thing ... indeed it's the best thing about us.**
St. Augustine

What keeps you awake at night when you ponder retirement? Why? Is it a real concern? Could you be overthinking?

By now you should have had a lot of aha moments. This, though, is a key journal question. Do not skip it.

Date: _____

_____

_____

_____

_____

_____

_____

_____

_____

_____

_____

_____

_____

_____

_____

_____

_____

_____

_____

_____

_____

_____

_____

_____

**All the world's a stage, and all men
and women merely players:
they have their exits and their entrances;
and one man in his time plays many parts,
his acts being seven ages.**
William Shakespeare

This journaling question actually involves drawing. It is a pictorial representation of where you are in life now. Go to page 146 to complete the Wheel of Retirement Assessment Tool. Once you are done, it will give you a portrait of your satisfaction levels and allow you to quickly and easily identify any areas that may need attention now.

Many of the previous journal questions should have given you some clarity around these areas. This exercise will give you some priority as to what needs attention before you retire.

In the next set of journal questions, you will explore how you can raise the level of bliss on each of these categories.

**Most of us spend too much time on what is urgent
and not enough time on what is important.**
Stephen R. Covey

What are the five biggest priorities you feel must be addressed before you retire? This can be nonfinancial and financial, for instance, how you will reduce credit card debt before retirement or how you can assist your children in establishing themselves in the world before you leave the workforce.

Discuss why each priority is important, how you have addressed this main concern, or when and how you will address each.

Date: _____

_____

_____

_____

_____

_____

_____

_____

_____

_____

_____

_____

_____

_____

_____

_____

_____

_____

_____

_____

_____

_____

_____

_____

**Remembering that I'll be dead soon is the most important tool
I've ever encountered to help me make the big choices in life.
Because almost everything—all external expectations, all pride,
all fear of embarrassment or failure—these things just fall away
in the face of death, leaving only what is truly important.**
Steve Jobs

Are you realistic about the timing of your retirement? Are you procrastinating, or are you accelerating your plans? Why?

Journal in detail why and how you are really feeling about the timing. Be honest. Keep the ego out of it. The Steve Jobs' quote is a bit severe, but it might help give some perspective. I put retiring in the "big choices" category.

Date: _____

_____

_____

_____

_____

_____

_____

_____

_____

_____

_____

_____

_____

_____

_____

_____

_____

_____

_____

_____

_____

_____

_____

Success is getting what you want; happiness is wanting what you get.
W. P. Kinsella

If this journaling process were a huge success, what would have to happen in the next year, three years, five years, and so on? Go out as far as you wish.

Date: _____

_____

_____

_____

_____

_____

_____

_____

_____

_____

_____

_____

_____

_____

_____

_____

_____

_____

_____

_____

_____

_____

_____

_____

_____

**It is common sense to take a method and try it. If it fails, admit
It frankly and try another. But above all, try something.**
Franklin D. Roosevelt, Looking Forward

Take a Trial Run

This next idea may not be practical in totality for you. Don't skip the next question. Really think about this one.

Is it possible for you to take a sabbatical? The definition is a rest from work, or a break, often lasting from two months to a year. Many firms and colleges require their employees to take a sabbatical every seven years or so. It takes a lot of planning because it is important to keep the high level of service while you are away. If your employer knows you are thinking of retiring, she or he may love the opportunity to see the holes that will need to be filled when you leave ahead of time. And a two-month sabbatical may be just enough to give you the feeling of what retirement will look like.

If you can't take a sabbatical, maybe a very long vacation would give you the same results. After many years of service, you may have five weeks of vacation. Would it be feasible to take it all at once?

Don't let your ego get in the way. Think, "How could my employer or business survive without me?" Remember the saying, "Nobody is indispensable."

So what do you think?

Date: _____

_____

_____

_____

JOURNAL YOUR WAY

PEOPLE IN YOUR LIFE

**People who think they know everything are a
great annoyance to those of us who do.**
Isaac Asimov

I'd like you to think about people in your life. Let's face it. Many of us have worked with the same people for years. The idea of never seeing some of these people again can be upsetting. Or the thought of seeing a person every day, all day, in retirement can also be interesting. You'll be resolving any concerns as you move through the journal. Don't run or suddenly decide you can't retire.

On the worksheet provided on page 148 or on these pages, make a list of the people you currently work with or regularly see because of work but won't see after you retire. For each person, indicate if you'll miss him or her, be happy you'll never see him or her again, or are neutral. And don't forget the maintenance man who has emptied your wastebasket for years. Include as many people as possible. The worksheet will help if you want to maintain a running list.

Date: _____

_____

_____

_____

_____

_____

_____

_____

_____

_____

_____

_____

_____

_____

_____

_____

_____

_____

_____

_____

**The best times we've had on earth
are usually with those we love.**
Van Harden

Make a list of nonwork-related people who you see on a regular basis, for example, spouse, friends, family members, neighbors, fellow volunteers, and so forth. A worksheet is provided later in this book.

For each person, indicate if you will see him or her more, less, or the same. Which people would you like to see more? Which would you like to see less?

Date: _____

_____

_____

_____

_____

_____

_____

_____

_____

**You can't change anyone else, but people do
change in relationship to your change.**
Jack Canfield

Will your relationship with any of the people in the previous questions change when you retire? If so, how will it change? And is it a good thing? If it isn't a good thing, how can you resolve this issue?

Date: _____

_____

_____

_____

_____

_____

_____

_____

_____

_____

_____

**Cherish your human connections—
your relationships with friends and family.**
Barbara Bush

Which relationships do you want to nurture and strengthen once you retire?
Who, when, and how?

Date: _____

_____

_____

_____

_____

_____

_____

_____

_____

_____

_____

_____

_____

_____

_____

_____

_____

_____

_____

_____

_____

_____

_____

_____

_____

_____

**How people treat you is their karma;
how you react is yours.**
Wayne Dyer

Will any of your relationships become vulnerable and need more of your attention when you retire? If so, who, why, and how will you handle this? What is the plan?

Date: _____

_____

_____

_____

_____

_____

_____

_____

_____

_____

_____

When you realize you want to spend the rest of your life with somebody, you want the rest of your life to start as soon as possible.
When Harry Met Sally (1989)

Describe new people who you would like to meet. What are their interests? What are you hoping to gain from the new relationships? How will you go about meeting these new people?

Date: _____

_____

_____

_____

_____

_____

_____

_____

_____

_____

_____

_____

_____

_____

_____

_____

_____

_____

_____

_____

_____

_____

_____

_____

I constantly work at maintaining balance. For me, my family comes first. If my family is taken care of, then everything else usually falls into place.
Faith Hill

Family Care Plan

Do you have family members who need to understand you will be retiring soon and will not be able to help them financially anymore or as much? It's so important to start the conversation early. Who will you speak with, what will you say, and when will you engage the discussion?

If you know this financial assistance will most likely continue from time to time, is that included in your financial plan? Do you have family members—your parents, siblings, and/or children—who will need assistance as they age due to illness and disability?

Do you have a plan? Have you had a family meeting about this assistance—in light of your upcoming retirement? What is the extent of the assistance? Will it impact where you and/or they live?

How will they be cared for when you pass or if you become ill? Is this assistance included in your financial plan?

For each family member or person you will have some responsibility for, financial or nonfinancial, when you retire, journal your ideas on how this will play out in retirement.

Date: _____

_____

_____

_____

_____

_____

_____

_____

_____

_____

_____

_____

_____

_____

_____

_____

_____

_____

_____

For me, family always comes first; I would do anything to protect them.
Mark Wahlberg

Protect the People You Love

Do you have a sound estate plan for when you pass? Nobody likes discussing this topic. You may be wondering why this subject is even in this book. If just one journaling person takes action on this topic, I'll be happy. Well, maybe more than one.

Honestly, it amazes me the number of people who procrastinate on this topic. Please do not. Dying without your loved ones knowing your wishes is really not fair to them, even if you think it is obvious. Having helped clients with the estate issues after their loved ones have died, I can attest to the difficulty.

Do you have, at the minimum, a will, health care proxy, and power of attorney? If yes, when was the last time you reviewed it? Do changes to the executor, beneficiaries, and/or trustees need to be modified? If you don't have the minimum estate plan, why? Please be honest!

Can you contact an attorney within a week or the next month? If not, when? Can you ask friends who they utilized as an attorney?

Date: _____

_____

_____

_____

_____

_____

_____

_____

_____

_____

_____

_____

_____

_____

_____

_____

_____

_____

_____

_____

JOURNAL
YOUR WAY

YOUR EVOLUTION

**One of the greatest regrets in life is being what others
would want you to be, rather than being yourself.**
Shannon L. Alder

The word "evolve" simply means to come forth gradually into being, develop, or undergo evolution. You have done a lot of thinking the past few weeks, and hopefully several light bulbs have gone off. It is time to take those thoughts and come up with an evolution retirement plan.

Susan Bradley, CFP®, CeFT™, a recognized thought leader in financial transitions planning, uses the term "reinvent yourself" during times of life transitions. I studied financial transitions under Susan for several years. Key questions she emphasizes to keep in mind for this reinvention/evolution plan are:

- Are you socializing?
- Are you challenging yourself?
- Can you measure your activities?
- Do you have some routines?

Socialize

Experts say it is important to socialize to maintain a healthy mind and body. It is important to include activities that include a form of socialization such as church, golf league, knitting club, and so on. *Psychology Today* says accumulating data on socialization may extend your life, help you enjoy better physical and mental health, and lower the risks of dementia.

Challenge Yourself

It is also important to have challenging activities. This keeps the mind and body healthy as well. Choosing challenging activities helps you grow as a person, gives you the feeling of being empowered, and helps you understand all you are capable of doing. Doing challenging activities that are right for you keeps you connected to humanity, and they keep your life from becoming too complacent and prepare you to deal with the unexpected. Examples include learning a new language, knitting, woodworking, cooking, and so forth.

It Should Be Measurable

Having goals that you must strive to attain is also good for the mind and body, even if it isn't a physical activity. It actually produces that good feeling. It doesn't have to be a physical measurement such as the number of Zumba classes attended. It could be the number of bridge games you have won this past month. Are you noticing a theme? When you consistently measure the results of something, your tendency is to get better at that activity.

It Should Be a Daily or Weekly Routine

You are just coming off many years of the workday routine. You may initially say, "I don't want any mandatory tasks or routines." That is fine for a while after you retire, but studies have shown that having some structure is just good for your overall well-being. Having routines is great because you don't have to constantly plan your day each day. It is already scheduled. Routines help you form good habits, become proficient in something and organize your life, and they can also provide direction.

The next several journal questions will help you reinvent your life to be the most you can be. I know you will experience many aha moments and light bulbs will be going off in your head.

This section is my favorite part of the book. All your hard work journaling about things that maybe were not so easy to do will now come together.

At the end of this book, a worksheet on page 145 will help you put it all together. If a question asks you to think of activities, transfer those activities to the worksheet. For instance, if you want to play bridge on Tuesday and Thursday evenings, "playing bridge" would be an activity you would want to capture. Is it social? Yes. Is it measurable? Yes. Is it a routine activity? Yes. Is it challenging? Yes.

Another example would be drinking coffee each morning while reading the paper. Is it social? No. Is it measurable? Not really. Is it a routine activity? Yes. Is it challenging? Not really.

Ultimately you want to have a good number of activities that fit all the categories. But depending on your personality, you may have many that do not have all four qualities. And that may be okay. Just keep in mind that neuroscience is leaning toward the benefits of all four qualities to keep us healthy, both mentally and physically.

We are all born with a unique genetic blueprint, which lays out the basic characteristics of our personality as well as our physical health and appearance ... And yet, we all know that life experiences do change us.
Joan D. Vinge

Unleash Your True Personality

I recently read the book *Quiet* by Susan Cain. She explains that, since the industrial revolution, our country has revered extroverts. Parents drilled into their introvert children that they needed to be more outgoing to get ahead. High schools, colleges, and businesses continued to promote this thinking. Then in the 1990s, different tests like the Myers-Briggs came to the forefront to help businesses understand the variety of their employees' personalities to form more effective teams.

But for many of us introverts acting like extroverts, it was too late. We really thought we were extroverts. After retiring recently, I took another personality test with no pressure from employers. I was a little surprised that I had several introvert tendencies. This was not a bad thing. I was actually thrilled. It explained the continued stress I had in my life trying to be what I really was not.

My point to this story is: have you been pigeonholed in a job for thirty-five to forty years that didn't fit your personality? Have you been an analyst or bookkeeper for thirty-five years when you really would have been happier in sales or a more creative job? Have you been in sales for thirty-five years when you would have been happy as a computer IT person writing code? Guess what? That is going to be over once you retire. You will be able to totally unleash your true personality.

An online free personality test is available for you at www.quietrev.com/the-introvert-test. After you take the test, please journal about your results.

Were you surprised? Does it describe you perfectly? Were you in the wrong job for your personality the past thirty-five years?

Do your friends and family expect a certain personality? Think about this.

What do you think your personality test means for your retirement? Can you think of activities you might like to try that you dismissed previously?

Date: _____

_____

_____

_____

_____

_____

_____

_____

_____

_____

_____

_____

_____

_____

_____

_____

_____

_____

_____

_____

_____

_____

_____

_____

_____

_____

**Don't you wish you could take a single childhood memory
and blow it up into a bubble and live inside it forever?**
Sarah Addison Allen

List five of your most cherished childhood memories. Then list three activities from childhood that you might be able to incorporate into your retirement plan. It can be as simple as picking blueberries.

Date: _____

_____

_____

_____

_____

_____

_____

_____

_____

_____

_____

_____

_____

_____

_____

_____

_____

_____

_____

_____

_____

_____

_____

_____

_____

_____

Personality is an unbroken series of successful gestures.
F. Scott Fitzgerald

What five words describe yourself? Can you think of any activities that would enhance your personality? Are there any activities or opportunities that could benefit from your participation because of your personality?

Date: _____

_____

_____

_____

_____

_____

_____

_____

_____

_____

_____

**A man who dares to waste one hour of time
has not discovered the value of life.**
Charles Darwin

In case you could not think of any words to describe yourself in the last question, here are some words that may help or add to your list. Choose three life values or personalities from this list. Why are those values important to you? How will you incorporate them into your life when you retire?

- Achiever
- Authoritarian
- Adventurer
- Friend
- Hero
- Independent
- Health nut
- King
- Pleasure-seeker
- Prince
- Princess
- Queen
- Recognition seeker
- Servicer/caregiver
- Sidekick
- Wealthy
- Wise

Date: _____

_____

_____

_____

_____

_____

_____

_____

_____

_____

_____

_____

_____

_____

_____

_____

_____

**The ant is knowing and wise, but he doesn't
know enough to take a vacation.**
Clarence Day

What were your favorite vacations of your lifetime? What are your dream vacations? Is it financially feasible to continue with the favorite vacations and the dream vacations? If not, is there any wiggle room? Can you juggle priorities? Do you have a once-in-a-lifetime trip on your mind? Would you take this trip early in retirement?

Date: _____

_____

_____

_____

_____

_____

_____

_____

_____

_____

_____

_____

_____

_____

_____

_____

_____

_____

_____

_____

_____

_____

_____

_____

When you're finished changing, you're finished.
Benjamin Franklin

Previous Life-Changing Events

Think back to major life-changing events you have experienced over the years, such as getting married, having a baby, going off to college, getting a divorce, going through the deaths of family members, and so on. Journaling about this is important because retirement is a major change. It would be great to know how you handle major changes in your life.

For each event, describe how you handled it. Did you hibernate from friends and family? Did you procrastinate on issues? Were you unable to make decisions? Did you have a get-it-done attitude? Did your health decline? Or did you make rash decisions?

Once you know these traits, how would you eliminate any of the negative reactions to change that you typically exhibit? What are your positive characteristics you could purposefully incorporate into this time of transition?

Date: _____

_____

_____

_____

_____

_____

_____

Morning is wonderful. Its only drawback is that it comes at such an inconvenient time of day.
Glen Cook

How do you want to feel physically and mentally each day you wake up? How do you want to feel physically and mentally each night before you go to sleep?

Date: _____

_____

_____

_____

_____

_____

_____

_____

_____

_____

**Half of the troubles of this life can be traced to saying
yes too quickly and not saying no soon enough.**
Josh Billings

What do you always say yes to? What activities do you always say yes to?

What do you want to say no to, but never do? What would be the consequences of saying no or at least once in a while?

How can you incorporate better yes answers into your life?

Date: _____

_____

_____

_____

_____

_____

_____

_____

_____

_____

_____

_____

_____

_____

_____

_____

_____

_____

_____

_____

_____

_____

_____

_____

Choice by choice we spin life's straw into gold.
Christina Baldwin

Your Worry Quotient

It is important to control your worrying. Maybe "worry" isn't a verb you use in your vocabulary, but it is normal to have some angst when you start to contemplate retirement or are in the throes of leaving the workforce. Not only does worrying cause stress and physical problems, it can also manifest the one thing we are worried about.

Dr. Joe Dispenza, the author of *Breaking the Habit of Being Yourself,* has a method for controlling worrying. He has studied quantum physics extensively. Science has proven that our thoughts can show up as reality in our lives. So if you are constantly worrying, whatever the issues are, it is bound to happen. Your subconscious mind puts things in motion based on your thoughts. In Dr. Dispenza's book, he provides guidance on turning around negative thoughts before they manifest.

I'll use myself as an example. And, yes, it is good if you can have your spouse or friends help. I'll admit it: I have a tendency to worry. Thanks, Mom! I am constantly working on this because I have seen the positive results from this work.

As soon as I have a worrying thought, I immediately say to myself, "Change." And my husband will also say "change" when he hears me worrying out loud. I instantly recognize I am worrying and turn that thought around. I ask myself one question forthwith, "Do I have any control over the situation?" If the answer is no, I stop worrying. Well, most of the time.

What worries you? List all the issues, whether retirement related or not, that worry you or really give you angst today. Next to each worry, write whether you have any control over the situation. If you do have any, highlight that issue for further work. Is it an immediate concern? Are there any activities that you could add to your daily routine to help mitigate your worrying?

The goal of this exercise is to give you a method to reduce your worrying. I estimate that 40 percent of the list is beyond your control and gives you the opportunity to eliminate that worry from your psyche.

Date: _____

_____

_____

_____

_____

_____

_____

_____

_____

_____

_____

_____

_____

_____

_____

The nature of life is to change and seek greater happiness, purpose and connection.
Susan Bradley

Your Happiness Quotient

When you did the Wheel of Retirement, you rated your "happiness." No matter what you assessed your happiness, you can always improve. And believe it or not, 50 percent of your happiness is genetic; 10 percent relates to circumstances, wealth, career, and status of marriage; and 40 percent is connected to your thoughts, words, and actions. Wow! That is huge. That means you have the power to change your happiness quotient! And one way is to spend time each day being grateful.

List all the things for which you are grateful. Having a gratitude list is important. We don't give thanks enough for what we have. It could be as simple as being able to watch the birds at the feeder each morning.

List the things that are working well in your life today. Write down the things you will be grateful for in the future.

Date: _____

_____

_____

_____

_____

_____

_____

_____

_____

_____

_____

_____

_____

_____

_____

_____

_____

_____

_____

_____

_____

_____

_____

_____

_____

_____

_____

_____

_____

_____

_____

_____

_____

_____

_____

I had a very detailed retirement plan, and I feel like I've met every aspect of it: a lot of golf, a lot of carbs, a lot of fried food, and some booze, occasionally—I've been completely committed ... The results have shown.
Andy Roddick

You have many decisions to make between now and retirement. List some resources that might be good for you to take advantage of now or later to steer you toward an awesome retirement. Why would they be good? When should you get involved?

Gather and list the information now. Research resources online. Here is a partial list of ideas: retirement workshops, personal coaching, therapists, books, financial planner, attorney, CPA, and retired friends.

Date: _____

_____

_____

_____

_____

_____

_____

_____

_____

_____

For me, every day is a new thing. I approach each project with a new insecurity, almost like the first project I ever did. And I get the sweats. I go in and start working, I'm not sure where I'm going. If I knew where I was going I wouldn't do it.
Frank Gehry

Now that you have gone through several journal questions, go back to your journal and review what you documented about what you'd be doing to fill your days. In these journal questions, you wrote about your typical week in retirement and the themes of each month. Are you able to fill in any blanks now?

Date: _____

_____

_____

_____

_____

_____

_____

_____

_____

_____

_____

_____

_____

_____

_____

_____

_____

_____

_____

_____

_____

_____

_____

_____

The real man smiles in trouble, gathers strength from distress, and grows brave by reflection.
Thomas Paine

You have done a lot of soul-searching and reflection. Go back to your journal and review which three words described what retirement means to you. When you think of retirement now, which three words come to mind? Why? What has changed from the first day you picked up this book and today?

Date: _____

_____

_____

_____

_____

_____

_____

_____

_____

_____

_____

JOURNAL YOUR WAY

ALMIGHTY DOLLAR

When life changes, money changes, and when money changes, life changes.
Susan Bradley

Your Money Story

What is your money story? It is defined as how money has impacted and is affecting your life now. It is a history of how you have handled money, how you feel about money, the impact it may have had on your life decisions, your family legacy around money, and so on.

Does money flow through your hands like water? Are you a saver, never spending a dime? Do you spend money but have a budget to keep you from going overboard? Are you petrified of money and talking about it? Are you somewhere in between? This is an important question. Being honest about your money story could be the difference between a happy retirement and a stressful one.

I'm not going to say any money story is good or bad. But you need to be above board with this and determine if your retirement can handle your money story. And if you have a partner in retirement, what is his or her money story?

Let's face it. Money brings up several good and bad emotions. What drives most decisions is the emotional side. Journaling about these emotions will be empowering. You may have many aha moments as you go through this chapter. You may find that your true money story is very different from the way you portray yourself to your friends and family. The ego needs to take a backseat here.

Okay, let's get to it.

It is my opinion that a man's soul may be buried and perish under a dung-heap, or in a furrow field, just as well as under a pile of money.
Nathaniel Hawthorne

It is time to get your money story down on paper. Take several deep breaths before starting this journal question. Remove all distractions. The following questions may help you with this process:

1. How do you handle money now? Are you a spender, saver, or frugal one?
2. Are you or your partner in control of the money?
3. Do you have the need to control the money?
4. Do you bail out family and friends when they have money problems?
5. Do you worry about money on a regular basis?
6. Are you afraid to even talk about money?
7. Are you always struggling with credit card debt?
8. Are you afraid to spend money?
9. How did your family handle money? Was there a defining moment in your younger years when your family had money issues? Does that impact you even now?
10. Did your family always have plenty of money, and you always got what you wanted as a child?
11. Do you think you don't deserve to have money?
12. Do you think you are entitled to have money?
13. How will you handle money when you are retired?
14. What is your partner's money story?

Date: _____

_____

_____

_____

_____

_____

_____

_____

_____

_____

_____

_____

_____

_____

_____

_____

_____

_____

_____

Money might not buy happiness, but it sure is nice to have.
Anonymous

Everyone's money story has positives and negatives. The goal of this journal question is to ask yourself if you are willing to incorporate some of the positives in some money stories to even out your money story. Money can be a huge stressor. Dealing with issues before retirement is important. Maybe you are happy with your money story. I am sure there is something you can improve in your money story.

I highly recommend you have a financial advisor run your retirement numbers for you, if this has not already happened. Or run the numbers yourself if you are confident in the process. You will need some concrete data to mesh the logical part of money with the emotional part of money.

If you are a "budgeter" and have no flexibility in your budget (negative), could you maybe lighten up a bit and spend some of your savings to travel or dine out (positive)? Is it important to die with millions or to enjoy yourself now?

If you are a "spender" and enjoy life to the fullest (positive) but may run out of money before you die (negative), could you possibly use a debit card instead of a credit card to keep control of your spending? Could you have a budget and try hard to keep to it and review periodically? Could you work part time? If not, what will you do to keep from running out of money?

If you are the "go-to person" and have a family fund for helping out others in financial trouble (positive), will you be able to say no when your fund potentially runs low or has a zero balance (negative)? Could you set up a family care policy and stick to it?

If your money story is perfect for you and your partner, you are probably a "tweener." You have all the positive aspects of all the money stories. Really?

Be creative and honest in your journaling. What are the positive aspects of your money story? What makes you happy about it? Do any of the positive aspects actually cause issues with you and/or your partner?

What are the negative aspects of your money story? Why are they negative? Do any of the negative aspects actually make you happy? Do any of the negative aspects of your money story actually cause issues with you and/or your partner? How can you eliminate any stressors and negatives from your money story?

Are there money issues beyond your control? If so, what is the impact on your retirement? Can you put in controls and boundaries to prevent the issues from impacting your retirement?

Make a list of the next steps you will take to improve your money story to work with your retirement.

Date: _____

_____

_____

_____

_____

_____

_____

_____

_____

_____

_____

**He that is of the opinion money will do everything may
well be suspected of doing everything for money.**
Benjamin Franklin

In retirement, what will be the five most important benefits of money for you, for instance, being able to afford health insurance? Discuss each benefit in detail.

Do you need to make adjustments to your financial plan to address these important benefits?

Date: _____

_____

_____

_____

_____

_____

_____

_____

_____

_____

_____

_____

_____

_____

_____

_____

_____

_____

_____

_____

_____

_____

_____

_____

**I am opposed to millionaires, but it would be
dangerous to offer me the position.**
Mark Twain

Will there be a significant change in your income and/or expenses during retirement? How do you feel about this alteration?

Do you have control over the change in your income and expenses that will make any unpleasantness disappear?

Date: _____

_____

_____

_____

_____

_____

_____

_____

_____

_____

_____

_____

_____

_____

_____

_____

_____

_____

_____

_____

_____

_____

_____

_____

_____

The lack of money is the root of all evil.
Mark Twain

What three things in retirement could put a crimp into your financial retirement plan? Are they realistic issues or just worry taking over? What could you do to revise your plan to address these issues, for instance, increase your umbrella policy? It might be a simple fix you just have not contemplated until you journaled about it. Your advisors may have very simple solutions.

Date: _____

_____

_____

_____

_____

_____

_____

_____

_____

_____

_____

_____

_____

_____

_____

_____

_____

_____

_____

_____

_____

_____

_____

_____

Assets put money in your pocket, whether you work or not, and liabilities take money from your pocket.
Robert Kiyosaki

Are Your Assets Protected?

You may have enough investments and assets to give you a comfortable retirement for years to come. Are your assets protected? Are they shielded from the unexpected that could wipe out your assets and your comfortable lifestyle?

This is a good time to review your insurance with your agents. I don't believe in being insurance poor, but retirees can't start over if something serious happens and they are not insured. When you are thirty years old, it is okay to take chances.

I heard a story of a retiree who recently purchased a condo. There was condo insurance for the building and structural damage in the condo provided by the association, but the client did not have insurance for the contents of the condo or loss of use. This cost him thousands of dollars when a bad storm caused extensive damage.

Do you need earthquake insurance? Did you know that, if an earthquake causes extensive damage to your home, if you do not have earthquake insurance, you are not covered? I live in the Northeast. We get minor earthquakes periodically. But all it will take is a good one down the road to set my retirement plan back a bit. Consequently I have earthquake insurance. Generally, if the chances of an earthquake are low, the premium will be inexpensive as well.

Sit down with all your insurance providers to review your coverage on your assets. The question to ask is, "Are my assets sufficiently protected in light of my entering retirement and wanting to protect my assets since I cannot start over building them up?" They love this question. Dollar signs may show up in their eyes. Review their recommendations carefully, and run them by your financial advisor.

Insurances to Review: (enter the results of the review here)

Household

Vehicle

Umbrella

Health

Life

Disability (depending on your age)

Long-Term Care

Date: _____

_____

_____

_____

_____

My wallet is like an onion, opening it makes me cry.
Anonymous

Money Times Two

If you are in a relationship, whether married or living together, I don't have to tell you that money enters into the picture almost daily. It may be subtle, but it is there. That is why it is critical that both partners are involved with the retirement planning and attend all meetings with financial advisors and attorneys together.

Kathleen Burns Kingsbury, a wealth psychology expert, founder of KBK Wealth Connection, and the author of several books, including *How to Give Financial Advice to Women* and *How to Give Financial Advice to Couples* says, "Each of you has a unique money history, risk tolerance, and viewpoint on how best to invest and accumulate wealth. By attending meetings together, the likelihood your advisor will design a successful financial plan and long-term investment strategy increase tremendously."[i]

What do you admire about your partner financially? Why? If money were a mirror for you and your partner, what would it say to both of you?

Are there money issues you need to address before retirement? What are they? What frustrates you the most? Why do they need to be addressed? What could be the consequences if these topics are not discussed now?

Have you taken steps up to now to accept each other's money story? Will it work in retirement? What steps can you take together to address these issues in retirement?

Do you have a financial advisor or CPA who can lay out some number facts for you? Does it make sense to go to a couples' therapist?

If you can't resolve some of these issues, what do you need to plan for now? Will one spouse work longer than the other to accommodate the finance issues?

Please journal on all these questions. Do not skip.

Date: _____

---

[i] http://www.kbkwealthconnection.com/couples-and-money/couples-financial-advisor/

_____

_____

_____

_____

_____

_____

_____

_____

_____

_____

_____

_____

_____

_____

An ounce of practice is worth more than tons of preaching.
Mahatma Gandhi

Take a Practice Money Run

I often ask my clients who are nearing retirement to take a trial run. What? Yes, try it out to the best of your ability.

Determine what your income and expenses will be in retirement. Could you live within those parameters for six months, starting now? How do you feel about this trial? Many clients are in denial and refuse to try. Others dive right in by getting the budget done and living up to that plan.

How will you feel if this trial doesn't work too well? What adjustments to your retirement plan need to happen? I have one client who said, "As long as I can have my cigars, I can live with any adjustments!" Many people want to retire so badly they think they can give up whatever it takes. But one to two years into retirement, that determination to stick to a budget goes down the drain.

Journal honestly about this. This is your private journey.

Date: _____

_____

_____

_____

_____

_____

_____

_____

_____

_____

_____

_____

_____

_____

_____

_____

_____

_____

_____

_____

_____

_____

NEW BEGINNINGS

Every new beginning comes from some other beginning's end.
Seneca

It has been several weeks now since you started journaling your way to retirement. How does it feel? If you journaled through all the questions (and I hope so), then you should have a good idea what your retirement will start out looking like or maybe not.

The important outcome is that you were able to explore your thoughts and feelings surrounding retirement and identify areas that you may need to work on before you actually leave the workforce. If you were stuck in a drab retirement when you picked up this book, I am sure you have been able to take away one or two actions that will reverse or at least enhance your current retirement.

It is important to remember that retirement is a major life transition. Transitions mean change, which is difficult for most people, especially at the beginning. It can take months to years before someone gets his or her stride in retirement. Be gentle with yourself. The more you plan ahead for retirement, the easier the transition will be.

I have some family and friends who are in their eighties and nineties. And many have told me that the best years of their lives were between sixty and eighty.

It is up to you now. Don't wait for others to plan your retirement. Believe me, somebody will come along to try to fill in your time. Make sure it is time well spent.

I would love to hear about your experiences with this journaling book. Reach out to me anytime at joan@journalyourwayto.com.

Warmest wishes,
Joan Marie

JOURNAL
YOUR WAY

REFLECTIONS/MEDITATIONS

Litmus Test

Retirement planning is not always sequential or linear, and our plans aren't always going to be perfectly executed. You may hit bumps in the road from time to time and question your retirement plans.

The Litmus Test exercise is designed to give you a go-to process when you need to tap into your logical and emotional brain. I believe everyone has intuition and knows when a decision is or isn't right. But our and our family's egos, along with financial issues, can cloud the decision-making process. This exercise can be used for many different decisions that come up in your life. The Litmus Test will help you tap into that intuition at a moment's notice and serve you well throughout your life.

You will require a quiet space, free from all distractions. You can even record the exercise on your phone or another electronic device so you can keep your eyes closed. It is a guided exercise. Go outside and find a stone or a smooth object you can hold in one hand. You may have something in your home, like a marble, although connecting to the energy of the earth is preferred. A marble is the size you want.

Take several deep breaths. Write down your question or decision so it is very clear in your mind. Close your eyes and hold the smooth, round object in your hand. Take several deep breaths. Now I want you to think of a time when you experienced peacefulness and bliss by yourself, a time when you were "in the zone." Where were you, what were you doing, and when was it? How old were you? Keeping your eyes closed, recognize what physical sensations you feel in your body. Are you relaxed? Are you smiling? Do you have butterflies in your stomach?

Keep your eyes closed. Keep that physical sensation alive. You want to be able to recreate this feeling so it is important to remember the sensation. Now feel the stone or rock in your hand. Connect your blissful feeling with this rock.

Now think of your question or decision you are addressing today. How have your feelings changed? Are you maintaining that blissful state, or do you immediately go to a bad place?

If you are able to maintain the blissful state while thinking about this issue, you are probably on the right track. On the other hand, if you went to a bad place, then more work needs to be done on your decision process, or you need to abandon the decision completely.

As you utilize the Litmus Test, you will develop a keen sense of your intuition. Use this test to guide you in your life's decisions.

Date: _____

_____

_____

_____

_____

_____

_____

_____

JOURNAL
YOUR WAY

A WALK IN THE WOODS

Without leaps of imagination, or dreaming, we lose the excitement of possibilities. Dreaming, after all, is a form of planning.
Gloria Steinem

Imagine you are walking up a trail in the forest that leads to the ocean. You stop to admire the waves hitting the rock formations off in the distance. It is so hard to continue because of the beauty and serenity of this vista. You don't want to turn around, but you don't want to go forward on the trail either. You are perfectly content right here and right now.

Look down the trail you have just walked. Recount the most important lessons you have gathered from your life experiences. Then look ahead on the trail. Are there lessons to learn as you go forward in life?

Date: _____

_____

_____

_____

_____

_____

_____

_____

_____

_____

_____

_____

_____

_____

_____

_____

_____

_____

_____

_____

_____

_____

EVOLUTION ACTIVITIES WORKSHEET

Date: _____

Activity	Is It Social	Is It Measurable	Is It a Routine	Is It Challenging

WHEEL OF RETIREMENT

Wheel Of Retirement Assessment Tool
(Before Retirement)

INSTRUCTIONS

Purpose of the Wheel of Retirement Assessment Tool:

- It may identify areas of your life that may need attention now, before or during retirement.

- If you are on the fence about retiring, it may push you over the fence.

- If you really want to retire NOW, it may help you see that you need to wait a bit.

- It may identify where you need more balance in your life whether you retire or not.

Tools you will need:

- A pencil
- A dark magic marker or crayon

Instructions:

- Print off the Wheel and instructions or you can draw your own wheel with the categories.

- Using the definitions and thought prompts of each category of the Wheel, score your satisfaction levels against each of the different categories using 10 as euphoria and 1 as tension (see example).

- Use dark magic marker to graphically highlight your scores. This will quickly show you the areas you need to work on before retirement.

Example:

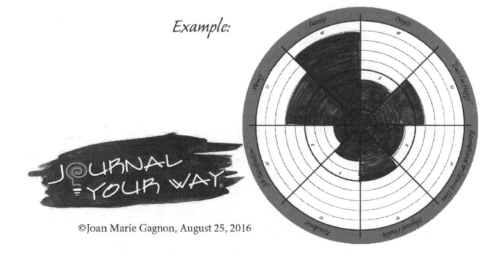

©Joan Marie Gagnon, August 25, 2016

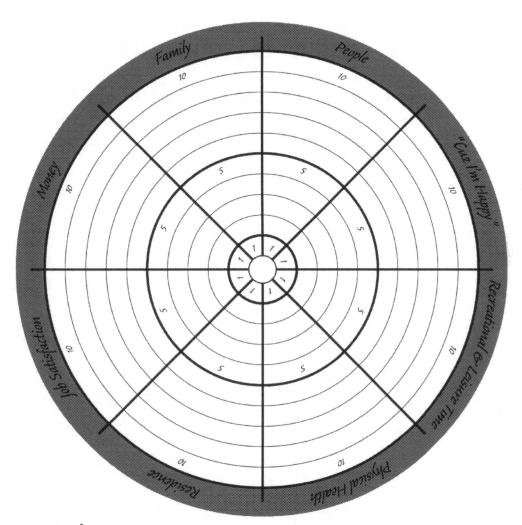

Wheel Category Definitions:

On a scale of one to ten, rank the areas of your life today before retirement. One represents complete tension and ten represents euphoria. The Inner ring zero and the outer ring is ten

Family ~ Do you spend time with your family? Are you always struggling to make time for your family? Do you have time to be supportive of your family?

People ~ Do you have a lot of people in your life other than your family and co-workers (i.e. friends, church community, exercise classmates, volunteer community)?

"Cuz I'm Happy" ~ How would you rate your happiness, in general?

Recreation and Leisure Time ~ How would you score the amount and quality of your recreation and leisure time today?

Physical Health ~ How would you score your physical health today?

Residence ~ Will you retire in your current home? Is it appropriate? Do you have a plan for where you will live in retirement if it isn't your current home?

Job Satisfaction ~ How would you rate your job satisfaction today?

Money ~ Have you met with a financial advisor to evaluate if your savings will support you in retirement? Have you been saving for some time now and built up a nice nest egg? Do you have a pension?

PEOPLE AT WORK WORKSHEET

Directions: List as many people as you can think of from work.
Then, determine if you will miss them. Do you miss them enough
to stay connected? If so, ideas for staying connected?

Name	Will Miss	Won't Miss	Want To Stay Connected	Ideas for Staying Connected

NONWORK PEOPLE WORKSHEET

Directions: List as many non-work related people you will be spending time with or want to spend time with on a regular basis.
Indicate if you will see them more or less in retirement than before.

Name	See More	See Less	See the Same	"Love" to See More	"Love" to See Less	Will Relationship Change when you retire

FURTHER READINGS

Breaking Money Silence: How to Shatter Money Taboos, Talk More Openly About Finances, and Live a Richer Life by Kathleen Burns Kingsbury

Breaking the Habit of Being Yourself: How to Lose Your Mind and Create a New One by Dr. Joe Dispenza

Quiet, The Power of Introverts by Susan Cain

Write It Down, Make It Happen, Knowing What You Want and Getting It by Henriette Anne Klauser

Sudden Money: Managing a Financial Windfall by Susan Bradley and Mary Martin

Joan Marie Gagnon is a Certified Public Accountant and a Certified Financial Planner ™ with thirty years of experience in the financial arena.

As a financial advisor, she noticed that, when individuals were getting ready to retire, it wasn't just the money they were worried about, especially if their work were their life. If they didn't work, what would they do? Having studied financial transitions, she knew that retirement would be very challenging for some of her clients. Hence, the idea of a book, *Journal Your Way to Retirement*, was born.

She actually retired a bit earlier than planned in 2016 and felt the stress and anxiety associated with being pulled into a different reality overnight. So she started journaling and found that it was a huge help in the transition. Since then she has expanded on those initial retirement journal questions for you to form a complete circle starting before retirement and ending in a blissful retirement. Joan Marie lives with her husband and their two dogs in Mansfield, Massachusetts.

Printed in the United States
By Bookmasters